Humans, after all

Verses from the Heart and Soul

DIVIT

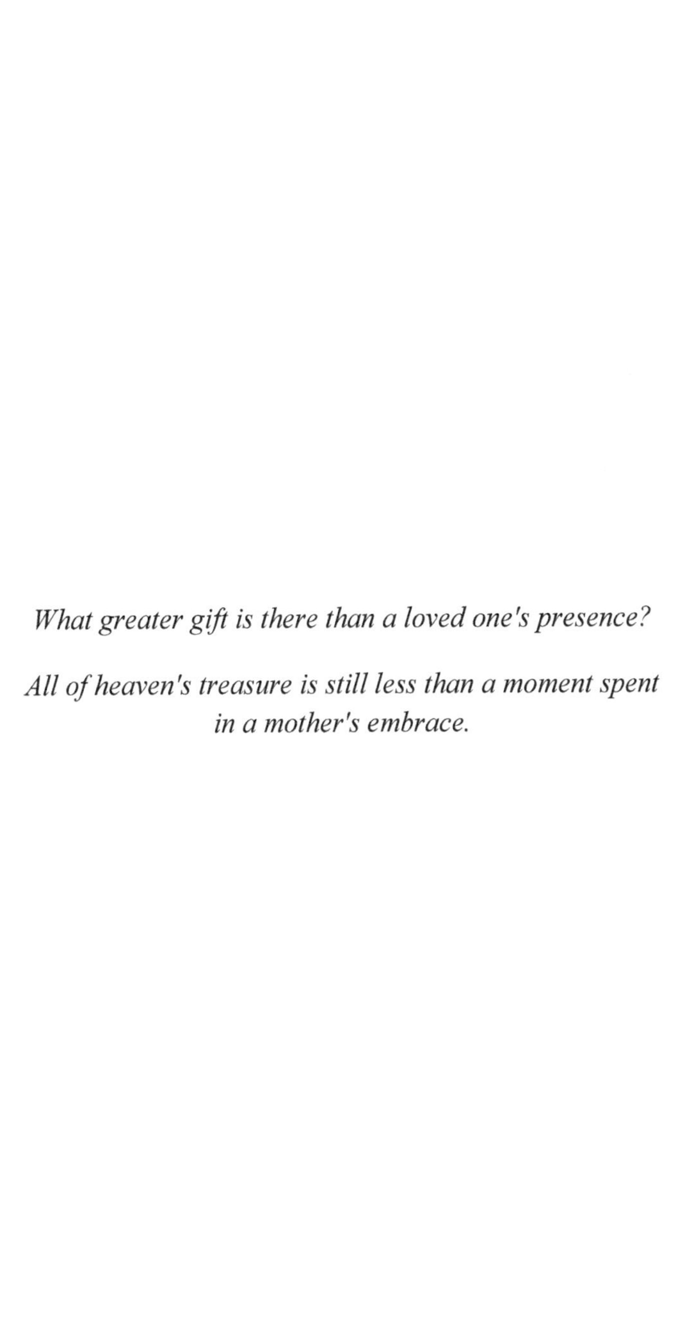

What greater gift is there than a loved one's presence?

All of heaven's treasure is still less than a moment spent in a mother's embrace.

Contents

CONTENTS

Preface

Poetry has always been a reflection of life—its beauty, its pain, its lessons, and its mysteries. This book is not just a collection of poems; it is a journey through emotions, experiences, and the unseen corners of the soul. Each piece is a moment captured in words, a feeling translated onto paper.

The inspiration for this book came from personal reflections, everyday observations, and the raw emotions that shape our existence. Writing these poems was both a cathartic and transformative experience for me. Some were born in moments of solitude, others in the chaos of life. Together, they form a tapestry of thoughts and emotions that I hope will resonate with you.

The essence of poetry lies in its ability to connect us—to our own feelings, to each other, and to the world. As you turn these pages, I invite you to find your own meaning in these words, to reflect on your own journey, and to embrace the emotions that make us human.

This book is for those who have felt deeply, for those who have loved, lost, and found themselves in between. May these poems be a source of comfort, inspiration, or simply a reminder that you are not alone in your experiences.

Divit
27 Feb 2025

Acknowledgments

Writing this book has been a journey filled with reflection, learning, and growth, and I am deeply grateful to those who have supported me along the way.

First and foremost, I want to thank **Shiny H.** for being my guiding light, a source of inspiration, and an unwavering presence throughout this creative endeavor. Your encouragement and belief in my words have meant more than I can express.

To my family and friends—thank you for your love, patience, and for always standing by me, even when I disappeared into the depths of writing. Your support has been invaluable, and this book would not have been possible without you.

A special thank you to every reader who takes the time to engage with these poems. Whether they bring you comfort, reflection, or a sense of connection, I hope these words resonate with you in some way.

Lastly, I am grateful for the journey itself—the moments of doubt, the bursts of inspiration, and everything in between. Writing this book has been an experience of self-discovery, and I am honored to share it with you.

Introduction

Poetry has always been a way to express emotions that words alone often fail to capture. This book is a collection of real-life poems—each one inspired by personal experiences, reflections, and the unspoken emotions that shape our lives. These verses explore love, loss, strength, fear, and the many complexities of the human soul.

The motivation behind this book was simple: to give voice to emotions that often go unheard. We all experience moments of doubt, heartbreak, resilience, and hope. Through poetry, I have tried to capture these fleeting emotions in a way that resonates with the reader. Whether you are seeking solace, understanding, or simply a connection to something familiar, I hope these poems offer you a sense of belonging.

This book does not follow a rigid structure—it is meant to be read in moments of reflection, whenever you need words that echo your thoughts. Some poems may bring comfort, while others may stir emotions long buried. My intention is not to dictate how you interpret these words, but to invite you to find your own meaning within them.

Life is a journey of emotions, and poetry is one of the purest ways to navigate it. Thank you for allowing me to share this journey with you.

1. Fake Love

Like trees in winter, cold and bare,

I stood in trust, without a care.

You bloomed like spring, all full of light,

But hid the darkness out of sight.

Your words, like leaves, fell soft and sweet,

Yet underneath, were lies discreet.

I gave my roots, my soul, my time,

While you pretended, played the mime.

Now I am stripped, left in the rain,

A heart that breaks beneath the strain.

Your fake emotions left their mark,

Like scars carved deep into the bark.

I ache like branches bent and torn,

By love that died before it's born.

Now left to face the storm alone,

A hollow heart turned into stone.

Now stronger, roots run deep and wide,

No longer swayed by shifting tides.

I stand tall, with scars to show,

From broken trust, I learned to grow.

2.Fear

Fear is like gravity, constant and near,

Pulling us down, grounding dreams here.

It weighs on the spirit, pulls at the soul,

Keeps us from climbing, achieving the whole.

Think of the stars, distant and grand,

Planets and worlds we can't touch by hand.

If fear were the force that held us in place,

We'd never have traveled to meet outer space.

Fear, like gravity, whispers, "Stay low,

This is your orbit, no further to go."

But rockets defy it, they break through the hold,

Fueled by a vision, by courage made bold.

When courage ignites, a force comes alive,

Breaking through barriers, daring to strive.

Just like the force that propels us to Mars,

It's the courage to rise that lets us touch stars.

So shed the fear, the gravity's lie,

Let it fall earthward, while you learn to fly.

For big things are found beyond that tight tether,

Where fear falls away, and dreams soar forever.

3.Dependency

We lean on others, day by day,

In ways so small, they slip away—

A friend's warm voice, a guiding hand,

The comfort of a close-knit band.

Dependence keeps us safe and near,

A quiet bond, both soft and clear.

But sometimes in that cozy bind,

We close the door on our own mind.

To think alone, to dare, to see,

Means loosening threads—just slightly free.

Not cutting ties, but finding room

To let our quiet thoughts bloom.

So hold the hands that help you grow,

But make the space to gently sow

The seeds of thought that are your own—

And find the courage to stand alone.

4.Suffering

Can you feel it—the weight in the air?

The quiet ache, the silent despair.

A friend smiles wide, yet breaks inside,

A stranger stumbles, with no one to guide.

Their laughter's hollow, their strength a show,

A river of pain we choose not to know.

Eyes plead softly, though words won't start,

A scream for help wrapped tight in a heart.

Do you remember your darkest night?

The crushing load, the fading light.

Someone saw you—or maybe they turned,

And the fire inside you dimmed or burned.

Now think: who's waiting, lost and unseen?

What would you give to change what has been?

A touch, a word, a moment to care,

Could break their chains, lift despair.

Feel their cry—it's yours, it's mine.

In every heart, we're intertwined.

To love, to help, to see, to stay—

Could save a life in the smallest way.

24

5.Loneliness

A quiet echo fills the room,

A shadow cast by endless gloom.

No hands to hold, no voice to hear,

Just whispered doubts and creeping fear.

The world moves on, a bustling stream,

Yet here I stand, caught in a dream.

The silence grows, a heavy weight,

A constant knock at an unseen gate.

The nights are long, the days are slow,

A fragile heart left to follow the flow.

Conversations fade, connections thin,

Loneliness lives where love has been.

Eyes meet screens but not the soul,

An empty scroll, a fractured whole.

A thousand faces, none that stay,

Loneliness walks with me each day.

But in this hollow, soft and bare,

I find a strength that's hidden there.

A place to breathe, a chance to mend,

To be my own, to be my friend.

For loneliness, though sharp and cold,

Is a story waiting to be told.

It's where the roots of courage grow,

A well of strength, a seed to sow.

So if you feel this aching hue,

Know someone else is feeling it too.

Loneliness binds us, yet sets us free,

A fragile thread of humanity.

6.Mindset

You like someone, they don't feel the same.

You try so hard, but still lose the game.

It hurts inside, a quiet ache,

A heavy heart, a path you take.

Life feels harsh, unfair, unkind,

Dreams slip away, you fall behind.

But even in pain, you choose to stay,

Living through struggle, day by day.

Not every effort will lead to a win,

But strength is built from deep within.

Keep going forward, no matter the fight,

The darkest paths lead to the light.

7.Denial

It's a strange kind of pain, isn't it?

To watch others chase what you once wanted but never had.

The dream that slipped through your fingers,

The opportunity you missed,

The life you imagined but never lived.

And yet, when the younger ones come, full of hope,

Eager to climb where you stumbled,

Why does it feel easier to stand in their way?

To say, "I struggled, so should you."

To deny them the chance you wished someone had given you.

But what does that truly solve?

Does their failure ease your regret?

Does holding them back rewrite your story?

The truth is, by withholding your help,

You don't punish the past—you poison the future.

You create a world where dreams remain dreams,

Where potential goes untapped,

And bitterness becomes the legacy you leave behind.

But imagine this:

What if you become the hand, you once needed?

What if you used your lessons—not as a barrier—but as a bridge?

What if you lifted someone higher,

So, they could reach where you could not?

Their success is not your failure.

It is a light, rekindled from the embers of your struggle.

It's proof that the path can be better,

That your story, though incomplete,

Can become the foundation of something greater.

So let go of the resentment.

Be the guide you wish you'd had.

Because in helping others rise,

You heal your own wounds,

And turn what you lost into a gift that lives on.

8.Rain

When hope feels lost, and skies turn gray,

The rain will wash your pain away.

Each drop, a promise, soft and true,

That life will always start anew.

The earth still blooms through storm and strife,

So will your heart, so will your life.

Let rain remind you, calm and slow,

Even the darkest clouds let go.

9. Reverie

In reverie's grasp, the mind takes flight,

Escaping the world, avoiding its fight.

Dreams of power, of fame, of more,

Yet the heart feels empty at its core.

Psychology speaks: the mind deceives,

Chasing illusions, ignoring what it needs.

Connection, kindness, a life that's real,

Not fleeting dreams but love to feel.

Awake, and act, let reverie guide—

Not to escape, but to turn the tide.

Dreams will fade, but the truth will stay:

Your choices shape your life each day.

10.Self-care

Life will fall apart sometimes. Plans will crumble, people will leave, and

nothing will make sense. In those moments, choose yourself.

Drink water, even if it feels pointless. Eat, even if you have no appetite. Rest,

even if your mind is racing. Step outside, even if the world feels overwhelming.

Self-care isn't about fixing everything—it's about surviving the storm. It's about

showing up for yourself when no one else does.

When life spirals out of control, anchor yourself in small acts of care. These

moments will not fix everything, but they will keep you standing until the storm

passes.

11.Silence

There is a bittersweet truth in silence:

the pain of unspoken feelings and the ache of unresolved distances.

It's the weight of what could have been said,

the conversations left unfinished,

the moments where words could have bridged the growing gap but didn't.

Yet, within this pain lies a quiet hope.

Bonds don't truly break—they falter, they fade,

but they wait.

If communication finds its way back,

if words are spoken again,

the relationship can breathe,

the distance can close,

and what felt lost can be found once more.

Because it was never truly "over."

12.Self love

We fall for others, we give our all,

Build dreams together, feel ten feet tall.

We think their love will never fade,

But time reveals the truth, delayed.

They leave, they change, or drift away,

And we are left to face the day.

Through tears and pain, we come to see,

The only love that sets us free.

In the quiet of loss, a truth is found,

Our own hearts are where we're bound.

For the world may change and people part,

But we survive by loving our heart.

In the End, We Love Ourselves Only

13.Overthinking

The Spiral and the Key

My mind spins tales, a ceaseless fight,

Each thought a shadow in the night.

I dwell, I doubt, I overplay,

And watch my peace slip away.

But here's the truth I've come to see:

Overthinking holds no key.

To break the cycle, I take control—

Act, don't dwell; live whole.

Name the fear, let it unwind,

Breathe the present, free the mind.

The spiral ends when I begin,

To trust myself, and look within.

14. The Moon Follows You

When darkness falls and shadows play,

The moon will guide you on your way.

A silent friend, forever near,

Its light will chase away your fear.

No step you take is yours alone—

The moon reminds you, you've a home.

15. Thoughts and Mindset

Thoughts are the sparks, fleeting and free,

Ideas that drift like waves on the sea.

They question, they wander, they often explore,

But without a guide, they're just scattered lore.

Mindset is steady, the anchor, the ground,

A choice of focus where strength is found.

It takes those thoughts, aligns them with care,

Turning intention to actions rare.

Thoughts can imagine, but mindset applies,

It faces the storms, it never denies.

For to achieve, they must intertwine—

Thoughts inspire, and mindset refines.

16.Respect

A friend brings laughter, a bond to share,

But a lover brings respect, beyond just care.

They value your dreams, your voice, your place,

And honor your need for personal space.

A friend may stand by, through joy and strife,

But a lover respects the balance of life.

They give you freedom, yet stay near,

Building trust, not ruled by fear.

Without respect, love cannot grow,

It fades like a flame without a glow.

But with respect, love stays strong and true—

A lasting bond for both of you.

17.Emotions

I give my time, my heart, my soul,

Yet feel no closer to feeling whole.

Their hands reach out, their voices plead,

But once fulfilled, they see no need.

Each day I toil, each night I bend,

But kindness rarely earns a friend.

In the rush for more, they fail to see,

The silent weight that's crushing me.

Still, I rise, though the world's unfair,

Carrying burdens they'll never share.

For though they take, and seldom give,

I'll choose to care—that's how I'll live.

18.Depression

The weight of plans left undone

pressed heavy, dragging each day into shadow.

Dreams sat idle, mocking me,

their silence feeding the ache inside.

Depression wasn't loud—

it crept quietly, stealing purpose,

turning hope into a distant blur.

I waited for change, but change never came.

Then I moved—slowly, deliberately,

facing each task I had long ignored.

The smallest win cracked the dark.

Momentum followed, and with it, light.

The answer was simple, though never easy:

Do the work. Build the life.

The climb was mine,

and so was the freedom.

19.Gratitude

Give with care, but guard the scale,

For endless giving can often fail.

When you give beyond what you receive,

They may forget, or worse, deceive.

Kindness too far may lose its grace,

And leave you in a thankless space.

To keep respect, let balance stay,

Or be taken for granted, day by day.

Give with love, but know your worth,

For equal ties hold true in mirth.

In measured giving, bonds will last,

A future built, not lost to the past.

20.Regret

Don't try to fix every mistake,

For some won't see the effort you make.

Their value for it may not remain,

And you'll be left with only pain.

Instead, let the lesson shape your mind,

To avoid the error next time you find.

The past can't change, but you can grow,

And steer your path where wisdom flows.

Fix what you can, but don't despair,

If others fail to see your care.

The key is learning, not regret,

To build a future without upset.

21.Phases of Life

At six, he watched with wonder bright,

Cartoons alive, a child's delight.

At twenty, he learned to craft and create,

Building the worlds that shaped his fate.

Now thirty-two, it's his daily art,

Work for a living, but still from the heart.

Life whispered its wisdom: "Each phase is your own,

Find joy in the season, wherever you've grown"

Through time and change, one truth remains clear—

Every moment holds magic, if we choose to revere.

22. Time as Illusion

You say you have time, but do you, my friend?

A moment begins, yet it's gone by the end.

You chase the hours, grasping in vain,

But time slips past like falling rain.

The past is a memory, the future unsure,

The present too fleeting to ever secure.

You plan, you wait, you hope, you try,

Yet time moves on—you don't know why.

So if you must live, then live it now,

Not after the clock will allow.

For time's not yours, nor in your hand—

Just an illusion, like lines in sand.

23. The Narcissist's Dilemma

I need others to validate me. Their admiration fuels my self-worth, like air to a fire.

Without it, I feel empty.

But when they get too close, I fear exposure. What if they see through the

image I've built? What if they realize I'm not as grand as I appear? So, I push

them away.

Yet, once they leave, the emptiness returns. I need them again. And so, the

cycle repeats—seeking attention, fearing intimacy, never satisfied.

A loop I cannot escape, because the very thing I crave is the thing I fear the most.

24.Imperfection

If you expect perfection, you'll always despair,

No one is flawless, life isn't fair.

Focusing on what they lack or do wrong,

Will leave you feeling lost all along.

But shift your view, see what they give,

The kindness, the effort, the will to live.

Value their presence, the love they show,

And peace within you will start to grow.

True joy is found not in what is not,

But in cherishing all that life has brought.

Embrace the imperfect, let go of control,

And you'll find solace deep in your soul.

25.Coffee & Sunset

As the sun sets low, the world fades away,

With coffee in hand, I pause at the end of the day.

The warmth in my grip, the fading light,

Brings peace to my mind, makes everything right.

No need to think, no need to do,

Just being in this moment, calm and true.

The sunset and coffee, a quiet embrace,

Detached from the rush, I find my place.

26.Memories, My Friend

Memories walk beside me still,

Through quiet dawns and nights so still.

They hold my hand in gentle grace,

Soft echoes time cannot erase.

They sit with me in candle's glow,

And tell me tales of long ago.

In laughter bright or sorrow deep,

They are the friends I'll always keep.

Some wear the faces I have known,

Some stand in places overgrown.

Yet all remain, through thick and thin,

A part of me, a home within.

So when the world feels cold and wide,

My memories walk by my side.

Through every loss, through each hello,

They whisper, you are not alone.

27.Temporary

Like waves that kiss the fleeting shore,

Like autumn leaves that dance, then soar,

All things must change, all moments pass—

No dawn can make the night still last.

The rose must wilt, the fire fade,

The brightest stars dissolve in shade.

Yet in their passing, life is bright,

For knowing loss makes love shine white.

Would laughter ring if none could weep?

Would joy be deep if time could keep

Each moment locked, unchanged, the same—

A world untouched, without its flame?

It is the fleeting that gives worth,

The seasons turning birth to earth.

So cherish now, embrace the flow,

For beauty lives in letting go.

28.Mistakes

They hurt us once, they made us cry,

With careless words, with cold goodbye.

But now they see, now they regret,

They try to heal, to pay their debt.

With kinder hands, with softer tone,

They stand, afraid, yet not alone.

They treat us well, they try to show,

That they have changed, they've learned, they grow.

But still, we doubt, we turn away,

Ignoring all they do or say.

If once we wished they'd make things right,

Then why not see their newfound light?

29. Timing

The sun sets swift, a fading glow,

A fleeting fire we cannot hold.

Look away, just for too long,

And what was bright is now all gone.

Life moves the same, in quiet turns,

Yet we ignore the way it burns.

We wait too long, we chase too fast,

Forgetting moments never last.

But time rewards the ones who see,

Who trust its flow and let things be.

Not just to watch, but to align,

To live, to feel—the rhythm of time.

30.Patience

Patience is not the art of wait,

But the quiet strength to navigate.

It's staying calm when storms arise,

And trusting time will bring the prize.

Not rushing forward, not standing still,

But embracing life, with steady will.

For in each moment, as we grow,

Patience teaches us to truly know.

It's the silent power we hold inside,

That lets us endure, lets us decide.

In patience, we find the strength to be,

In harmony with life's mystery.

31.Bullying

They tried to dim your little light,

Called you wrong instead of right.

But stars don't ask the sky for space,

They simply shine with quiet grace.

So stand up tall, don't hide away,

Your spark was meant to light the day.

And when you see a heart that's blue,

Lift them up—let them shine too!

32.Deserve

They run toward dreams with fire in their eyes,

Not for the love, but for the prize.

Each step they take is proof they belong,

Yet deep inside, it feels all wrong.

They push and grind, they burn and break,

Giving it all, for success' sake.

But when they stand where they wished to be,

The joy is gone—it's empty.

The cheers, the praise, they come and fade,

Leaving behind a heart betrayed.

The spark that once had lit their way,

Now flickers weak, then dies away.

So off they go, to chase again,

A brand-new path, a different pain.

But in the end, the cycle stays,

A hollow chase through endless days.

Perhaps the race was never the key,

Perhaps the prize was meant to be

Not in the goal, not in the gain,

But in the love, not in the strain.

33.A path to one

I walked alone, my path was clear,

No ties to hold, no one near.

I chased my dreams, I forged my way,

No love to slow, no words to stay.

Yet in the silence, I could see,

Success felt cold with only me.

For what is life without a share?

A heart that loves, a soul that cares.

34.Judgments

I chase the ones who turn away,

Their silence calls, I beg to stay.

Yet those who stand with open hands,

I push aside like drifting sands.

I crave a grace, a form refined,

A softness shaped within my mind.

But when the world speaks loud and free,

It feels too raw, too wild for me.

Why can't I love what simply "is"?

Why must I mold, reshape, and dismiss?

Perhaps the fault is not in them,

But in the walls, I built within.

So let me learn, let me unbind,

To see with heart, not just the mind.

To take each soul as they appear,

Without the weight of love or fear.

35.Focus

Eyes on the prize, the goal in sight,

Through twists and turns, they find their light.

Not bound by one unchanging way,

They shift, adapt, but never stray.

They hear, they see, but filter well,

Ignoring noise that breaks the spell.

With heart so strong and mind so free,

They shape their path, their destiny.

36. Whispers of Imagination

Beneath the old oak, lost in thought,

A dreamer sat, the world forgot.

Eyes adrift in skies so wide,

Weaving realms where stars reside.

In golden castles, high and bright,

They danced with shadows, chased the light.

A place where sorrow dared not stay,

Where time and pain could melt away.

Yet voices called, soft but near,

"Come back, dear soul, there's wonder here."

For dreams alone can't shape the way,

Life must be lived, not dreamed away.

37.Unconditional Love

A child once cried in darkest night,

Afraid, alone, with fading light.

Yet arms so warm, so soft, so true,

Held tight and whispered, "I'm with you."

Years would pass, the child would grow,

Through love and loss, through joy and woe.

Mistakes were made, hearts were torn,

Yet love remained, though bruised and worn.

Not bound by rules, nor chained by fear,

Not lost in distance, always near.

Even when voices turned to stone,

The love still whispered, **"You're not alone."**

Unconditional—pure and wide,

A love that walks but does not hide.

It does not break, it does not bend,

It stands through time—it does not end.

But love is not to lose oneself,

Not pain to bear or quiet shelf.

It lifts, it shines, it sets one free,

Not as a cage, but as the sea.

So know this love, but guard it too,

For love should heal, not burden you.

And if you find it, let it stay—

A guiding light, through night and day.

38. Mirror

The way I speak, the way I care,

Reflects in life, it's always there.

A whisper soft, or words unkind,

Shapes the world within my mind.

If love I give to self each day,

Then kindness flows in what I say.

But if I scorn, or doubt my worth,

My fears take hold, my joy is dearth.

Decisions bloom from thoughts I keep,

Like steady hands or waters deep.

A soul at peace will choose what's right,

But fear can cloud the clearest sight.

The way I stand, the way I glow,

Shows the love I choose to show.

For if I treat myself with grace,

It shines upon my words and face.

63

So let me cherish, let me mend,

For how I love myself will send,

A ripple wide, a light so true—

That shapes the world in all I do.

39.Manner

They whisper soft, yet build a wall,

A silent cage, unseen by all.

They pull the strings, they shape the air,

And slowly steal the world I share.

They fear the voices I might hear,

The truth that may come ringing clear.

So doors are locked, the ties are tight,

They keep me hidden from the light.

Is it love, or is it chains?

A quiet rule, yet cold remains.

They say it's safe, they say they care,

Yet I am trapped, yet none are there.

Do they fear I'll find my way?

That I might rise, break free one day?

That I might see beyond their lies,

And learn to live with open skies?

For love is not a prison cell,

Nor shadows cast where silence dwells.

If care is real, it sets me free,

Not keeps the world away from me.

40.Life

Life stands before me, two roads unfold,

One bathed in fire, the other in gold.

Both call my name, both whisper dreams,

Yet neither is ever quite what it seems.

To take one path, I must leave another,

Like losing a love, like losing a brother.

A part of me stays where I cannot tread,

A shadow, a ghost, a wish left unsaid.

Desire is costly, the price is steep,

What I long to hold, I cannot keep.

To reach the stars, I must let go,

Of something I love, of something I know.

And so I choose, though my heart may break,

A single step that shapes my fate.

No turning back, no second sight,

Only the courage to walk through night.

For maybe life is not to keep,

But to lose, to love, to leap.

To pay the price and bear the scar,

To find out who we truly are.

41.Respect

Do not bow to age alone,

For wisdom isn't always grown.

Years may pass, but hearts stay cold,

Not all who age are kind or bold.

They were children, once like me,

Yet not all learn, not all see.

Some grow bitter, some grow blind,

Not every elder holds a mind

Of love, of truth, of guiding light,

Some only know to curse and fight.

So why should I give what they don't return?

Why should I love when they let me burn?

Respect is given where kindness stays,

Not just for those who count their days.

If you lift me, I'll stand by you,

If you guide me, I'll walk with you.

But if your words tear me apart,

I owe you nothing—not my heart.

So young or old, heed this plea:

Respect is earned, not forced from me.

42.Choice

The love you choose, like sun or rain,

Can bring you joy or endless pain.

A gentle hand, a voice so kind,

Can shape your heart, your soul, your mind.

A love that lifts, that lets you grow,

Will light your path with golden glow.

But love that wounds, that pulls you deep,

Can steal your dreams, your peace, your sleep.

A heart that's cherished learns to fly,

But one that's broken asks just why.

So choose with care, let wisdom guide,

For love can heal or crush inside.

Your life depends on whom you trust,

On love that's pure, on love that's just.

For in their arms, through storm or blue,

The life you live is shaped by who.

43.Chase

We chase the ones who turn away,

Who never call, who never stay.

Their silence makes us want them more,

A locked-up heart, a distant shore.

Yet standing near, through thick and thin,

A love so pure, yet left unseen.

A hand that reaches, soft and true,

Ignored, while chasing something new.

Is love the fire that burns so bright,

Or hands that hold through darkest night?

Is love the thrill, the fleeting high,

Or one who stays when teardrops dry?

Oh foolish hearts, why do we run,

From steady moons to chase the sun?

For when the fire fades to dust,

We'll find true love was built on trust.

44.Death

I love her now, with all I am,

But time moves fast like slipping sand.

One day, this touch, this voice, this face,

Will fade into a time and place.

One day, I will close my eyes,

No breath to speak, no words, no ties.

She'll stand alone, or maybe not,

But life won't pause—our love is caught.

And one day too, she'll fade away,

No one escapes, no one can stay.

The world moves on, no matter who,

No love, no bond can change what's true.

It's sad, it's real, it's how things go,

No fairy tales, just time's cold flow.

All we can do is love right now,

Before the clocks force their final bow.

45.Late

I had your heart, so full, so true,

Yet never gave the same to you.

I thought you'd stay, through every fight,

I thought love waits—was I not right?

I saw your eyes grow dim with pain,

Ignored the storm, dismissed the rain.

You whispered words I should have heard,

But I was blind to every word.

And then one day, you walked away,

No final plea, no wish to stay.

I reached too late, you turned to go,

The love I lost, I'd never know.

Now nights are long, the days feel cold,

I see the truth in stories told—

That love won't wait for careless hands,

It fades like footprints in the sand.

If I had known, if I had tried,

If I had fought instead of lied,

Perhaps today, you'd still be near,

Instead of just a ghost so clear.

46.Indifference

I used to flinch at every word,

A glance, a sigh, a rumor heard.

I let their whispers shape my days,

Their fleeting moods decide my ways.

But now I see, it's all a game,

A cycle spun with no one to blame.

Their actions? Theirs. Their minds? Their own.

Not my weight to bear, not mine to own.

I've learned to watch, not feel, not chase,

To meet cold stares with quiet grace.

No anger, no plea, no wasted breath,

No battles fought where silence rests.

Their judgments fade, their tricks grow weak,

For I've unlearned the need to seek.

Approval, praise, a hollow prize—

I see the truth behind their lies.

I walk away with head held high,

No storm can touch, no tear to dry.

Unshaken now, I stand alone,

For peace is found when cares are gone.

47.Return

You turn away, you close the door,

But life will bring it back once more.

The fear you fled, the path untread,

Will wait for you just up ahead.

A lesson dodged is not erased,

It finds new time, it finds new place.

Disguised in faces fresh and new,

Yet still it whispers, calling you.

You run, you hide, but still it stays,

In different forms, in different ways.

Until you stand, until you see,

That what you fear can set you free.

48.Change

No day remains, no night will stay,

The sun must rise, then fade away.

The storm that roars, so fierce and wild,

Will calm itself, soft as a child.

The pain you feel, the weight you bear,

Will shift and lighten through the air.

No sorrow lingers all life through,

For time will paint the skies anew.

So trust the wind, embrace the flow,

The darkest nights make bright stars glow.

Each dawn will bring a different hue,

And what was lost may come to you.

49. The Ghost of a Love That Never Was

I hear her voice, though she never spoke to me,

A distant echo, a melody free.

Not meant for my ears, yet I still listened,

In silence, in longing, in hope that glistened.

She was never mine, not even near,

A passing shadow, yet held so dear.

I reached with warmth, she answered cold,

Left me standing with stories untold.

Not once a memory, not once a touch,

Yet why does she linger in my thoughts so much?

Not love, not hate, but something in between,

A whisper of what could have been.

I told myself, "You can't force a soul,

To stay, to care, to make you whole."

Yet still, my mind won't set her free,

Though she never once thought of me.

Perhaps it's not her, but what she took—

A piece of my heart, a page in my book.

Not by love, nor loss, nor fate's cruel art,

But by the wound of an unanswered heart.

So I let her fade, like a song grown dim,

Not holding to ghosts, not longing for "when"

For love is not cold, love is not pain—

And she was just an empty name.

50.Embrace the Rush

Excitement swirls, so wild, so free,

A spark of joy, a rushing sea.

But breathe it in, don't chase, don't race,

Let it flow at its own pace.

Feel the thrill, but stand your ground,

In stillness too, the joy is found.

Epilogue

Time has a way of reshaping the stories we tell ourselves. What once felt like an ending becomes a mere pause, a breath between chapters. We move forward, carrying pieces of the past—some as lessons, some as scars, and some as quiet reminders of who we used to be.

Every word in these pages was born from reflection, from the raw moments that define us. Love, loss, fear, hope—they intertwine, shaping our journey. And yet, through all of it, we continue. We learn. We grow.

Maybe that's the real purpose of it all—not to avoid pain, not to chase perfection, but to embrace the temporary nature of things. To find meaning in the fleeting, to accept that nothing stays the same, and to trust that change is not the enemy but the very essence of life.

As you close this book, know that your story is still unfolding. Each sunrise brings a new verse, each choice a new direction. Whatever comes next, step forward with courage. The best chapters are yet to be written.